From Pouch to Couch

Why Lavender the Opossum Lives in a House

FERNCROFT
WILDLIFE RESCUE
Woodstock, CT

By Pamela A. Lefferts
Illustrated by Sara M. Lo Presti

Special Thanks:

Elisabeth Cotton for her energy, enthusiasm, and editing skills throughout this project

Lor Bingham, Editor, Calico Editing Service

Ferncroft Wildlife Rescue is a 501(c)3 Non-profit Organization
Federal USDA Class C Permit and CT DEEP Approved to house non-releasable educational ambassadors.
Permits to provide educational programs in CT, MA, and RI
Member: CWRA, NWRA, OSUS, NOS, NWF

Wildlife rehabilitators receive no State or Federal money and rely on donations to provide care for the animals.

From Pouch to Couch: Why Lavender the Opossum Lives in a House

Published by Ferncroft Wildlife Rescue 2021
Copyright © 2021 Pamela A. Lefferts and Ferncroft Wildlife Rescue

Printed in the USA

For permission requests, contact Ferncroft Wildlife Rescue at FerncroftWildlife.com

WOODSTOCK CT

LCN-2021905563
ISBN-13: 978-1-7368792-0-7 Paperback
ISBN-13: 978-1-7368792-1-4 Ebook
ISBN-13: 978-1-7368792-2-1 Hardcover

Photo Credits: Bill Blass, pages 33,37. All other photos Pamela A. Lefferts
Illustration Credit: Sara M. Lo Presti

In memory of Rudy, who taught us so much
and was a wonderful friend to Lavender.

"Birds should fly in the sky.
Fish should swim in the water.
Animals should run free
in the fields and the woods."

-Pam Lefferts

Hi, I'm Lavender! I'm an opossum.

My life had a shaky beginning, but thanks to a bit of luck and a lot of kindness from strangers, I have an incredible story and a very special job. Yes, I have a job! Want to know what it is? I can't wait to tell you about it…

Possum Or Opossum?

Did you know? O-possums and Possums are two different animals.

Possums live in Australia and are closely related to kangaroos.

O-possums are the Virginia Opossum and are the only marsupial that lives in North America.

O-my!

Bump

Bump

Bump

Ouch!

"Do you mind if I share?"

Sometimes animals of different species, like an adult opossum and a cat, can become friendly enough to share a bowl of food. Sometimes they may even shelter together for warmth. Opossums have a hard life in the wild, and are often seen sharing food with other animals.

It all started when my mom befriended a cat. One day, hoping to share some delicious cat food and a warm bed, my mom followed the cat into a house! I was safe in her pouch with my brothers and sisters. Suddenly Mom began to run up some stairs. I tried to hold on to her soft fur but I couldn't! I tumbled out from her pouch and bump, bump, bumped down the stairs.

Ouch!

Mom didn't notice I had fallen out! She carried on running and I was left alone. I found a cozy place by a radiator where it was warm and I waited for help.

Luckily, I was found by the owners of the house who knew exactly what to do to keep me safe.

AAACK!!!

«Move over! I was here first.»

An opossum mother's pouch has a strong muscle that allows her to close it very tightly. When a mother opossum is relaxed — when she is eating or sleeping — she lets her pouch open for fresh air. If she is frightened suddenly and does not have time to close her pouch, her babies, called joeys, can fall out or get lost.

"It is so bright out here."

FERNCROFT WILDLIFE RESCUE

Wildlife rehabilitators have to take classes and obtain special permits to take care of injured, sick, or abandoned animals with a goal of releasing them back to the wild.

The next thing I knew, I was blinking up at two very smiley faces. I had been taken to a special place called Ferncroft Wildlife Rescue.

"It's OK," the lady said. "This is a place where we help animals like you to get better and well enough to go back to the wild. I'm Pam and this is Bill."

Rehabbers Pam and Bill gave me food and medicine and put me in a warm bed, but I was lonely. I missed my mom. I was sad and didn't want to eat.

Then Bill had an idea. He made a soft cloth pouch for Pam to wear around her neck. "Here you go, Lavender," Bill said as he picked me up and placed me inside the pouch. It was warm and so comfortable – almost exactly like Mom's pouch. The motion of Pam walking and the sound of her heartbeat comforted me and I felt safe.

"You sound a lot like my mom!"

Baby opossums stay warm, snuggled in their mama's pouch for two months before they open their eyes. They are rocked to sleep by her motion and are calmed by the sound of her heartbeat.

Lavender

A proper diet for ambassador opossums like Lavender is very important to keep her healthy. Special foods and supplements are part of their daily meals.

I ate, I slept, and I grew. Pam fed me special milk from a tiny syringe and I stayed happily in the warm, soft pouch around her neck for almost a month! One morning I opened my eyes and looked out of the pouch. You should have seen the smile on Pam's face.

"She is so sweet," Pam said. "I'm going to call her LAVENDER." I liked the name Lavender.

So, I gave them each a name. From then on they were Mama and Papa to me!

Mama surprised me one morning – she left me a little saucer of milk. I looked around. The syringe was nowhere! I sniffed the milk. I sniffed again. Then I stuck my tongue out and felt it. Before I knew it, I was lapping away at it. Milk splashed on my fur and on my whiskers.

"She loves it!" Mama cried.

I did! I could feed myself without needing the syringe!

From that day on, I watched and learned. I found that I really enjoyed learning things so I always tried hard to listen. Ferncroft, the place where Mama and Papa lived and worked, had the important mission to rehabilitate opossums like me so that we may be returned to the wild, where we belong.

Rescue
Rehabilitate
Release

Wildlife rehabilitators try to help animals become healthy so they can be released back to the wild to be happy and free.

The rehabbers' motto is Rescue (save), Rehabilitate (make healthy), and Release (set free).

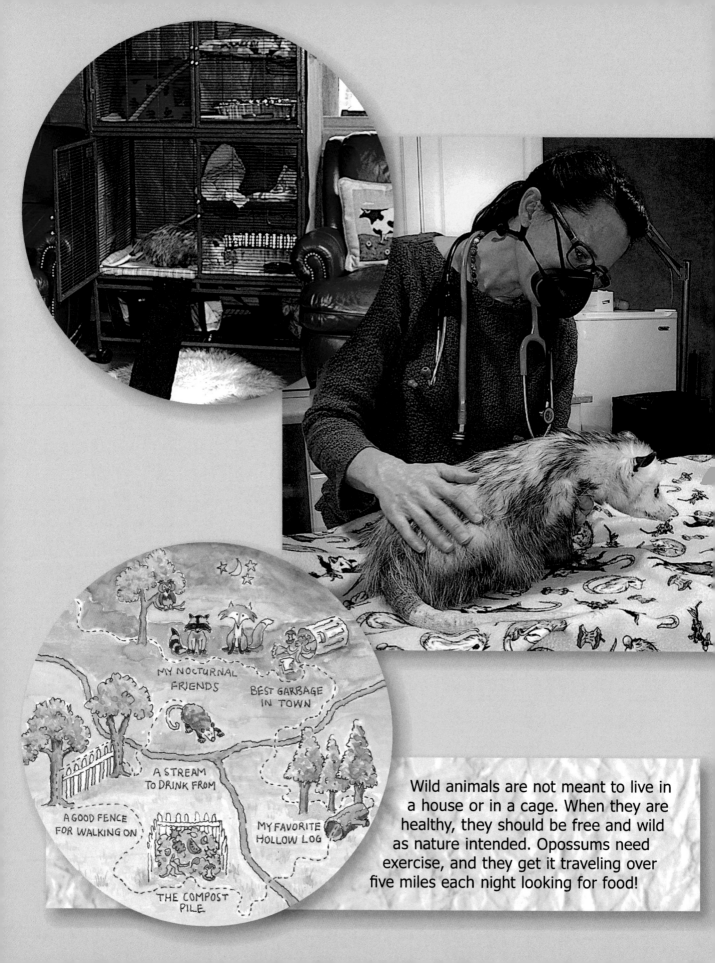

MY NOCTURNAL
FRIENDS

BEST GARBAGE
IN TOWN

A STREAM
TO DRINK FROM

A GOOD FENCE
FOR WALKING ON

MY FAVORITE
HOLLOW LOG

THE COMPOST
PILE

Wild animals are not meant to live in a house or in a cage. When they are healthy, they should be free and wild as nature intended. Opossums need exercise, and they get it traveling over five miles each night looking for food!

However, when we went to visit the veterinarian, I overheard her say that I should not be released to run free in the wild because my injuries left me without natural defenses. I didn't really know what that meant, but I didn't mind because Mama decided I would be their "forever opossum" and live with them forever!

Papa rolled a cage into the living room and I became part of the family. I learned how to use a litter box and how to climb out of my cage using a ramp. I also learned how to run on an exercise wheel.

I occasionally was treated to a warm bath. Some opossums do not like baths, but not me! After a shampoo and blow dry, Mama always cleaned my ears and trimmed my nails. When I left the Ferncroft "salon," my silky, soft fur smelled so sweet!

While my brothers and sisters were learning to root for grubs in the wild, Mama carefully prepared my meals. She made the best veggie omelets in Connecticut!

"Grubs! My favorite."

In their den in the forest, opossums groom themselves similar to how a cat does, by licking their fur or by licking their paws and rubbing them over their fur.

Wild opossums eat many different things to balance their diet. Grubs, lizards, mice, carrion, fallen fruit, and ticks are favorites.

"I said to back off, dog."

Dogs are a dangerous threat to opossums. Even the sweetest dog can injure opossums by trying to play with them. Rehabbers do not let opossums that will be released become friendly with their family dogs. Non-releasable opossums can make friends with the family pet.

One day, I heard Papa say that as they grow, opossum joeys begin to explore their world by venturing out farther and farther from their mother, until one day, when they are about five months old, they go off on their own.

I liked the sound of this and decided to set out on an adventure of my own!

I was feeling very daring and curious. There was a room I had never been in and I wanted to explore it. I knew I wasn't supposed to go in there but… well, a young joey has to have an adventure! When I crept inside the room, I saw a dog eating something. It smelled delicious and I couldn't resist. I hurried over.

"What are you eating?" I asked the dog.

"A bagel." She smiled at me. "I'm Destiny – you can have a bite if you like."

I didn't say no! I munched the bagel and felt so happy.

But then I heard a noise. Mama was in the room. I thought she would scold me, but she didn't. In fact, she laughed and took photos.

"You do know," Mama said to me that evening while I snuggled up on her knee. "If you were out in the wild, you would be waking up now, ready to start your day. Opossums sleep during the day normally and wake up at night." I couldn't believe that because I was the opposite; living in a human world, I was often awake during the day.

Every morning I played with Destiny the Dog. We had our breakfast and then would settle down for a nap together.

"I love staying awake all night long."

Opossums are nocturnal animals. In their natural habitat they are mostly active at night, although you may sometimes see a hungry mother looking for food during the day. They are most active from very late evening until just before dawn. You don't often see an opossum because while you're sleeping, they're playing.

Educational Ambassadors travel to classrooms and educational programs to teach the public about their species. Mama told me that Educational Ambassadors are very important.

Perfect Educational Ambassador

Happy Birthday Lavender

When my first birthday came, Mama had a big surprise for me.

"Lavender, it is time to teach you to be an Educational Ambassador. You'll have a lot to learn."

I had no idea what that meant, but I liked the sound of it and I loved learning things.

"But first of all, I have something to show you."

Mama had organized a big party for me! Over 100 people came to the center to meet me. There were tents, games, and a special birthday cake just for me! I loved all the attention.

"You will make the perfect Educational Ambassador," Mama said with a smile. It was the best birthday ever.

The hard work then began.

There was lots to learn, but Mama spent hours handling me so I got used to being petted, having my ears and tail rubbed, and showing off my pouch. I learned how to wear a harness and leash and how to ride in the car in my special travel cage.

"Lavender," Mama declared weeks later, "you are ready for your first public show!"

I was very excited but also a bit nervous. I hoped we had done enough training. We drove to the local library.

"Here is our Educational Ambassador, Lavender," Bill said. I shared my story with a group of children.

I was a hit! Everyone loved hearing all about me and I loved it when they petted me.

I felt so happy; it was the perfect job!

That was the beginning of my career, and I've been working hard changing hearts and minds ever since.

PET CARRIER

Opossums are not pets. They require
a very special diet and medical care.
They are happiest when allowed to run
free in the woods and the fields.

Opossums have "prehensile" tails. Prehensile means the ability to grasp and hold on. Opossums use their tail for balance when climbing and to gather leaves and sticks to make a nest.

I have lots of friends and even more fans, but they are *human* friends. I get to meet lots of volunteers and visitors who stop by to say hello.

I sleep in a soft, fluffy bed in a warm house. I can also curl up on Papa's lap, but my favorite place to nap is under the couch! I use my tail to carry my special blanket to the couch where I curl up most days.

But Mama reminds me I need to exercise.

"If you were in the wild," she tells me, "you would have a much harder life. You can't become lazy here or you will gain weight."

So I happily use the wheel and exercise every day. I love running on it and I have strong muscles and a healthy body.

I present many educational programs these days. Some are in person and some are virtual on the computer. I have a new partner, Patch, who is also a trained ambassador. Patch is sweet and gentle – and very big! Together, we go to schools, nature centers and special events. Everyone loves Patch. I also have a new baby sister named Bella who is as sweet as can be. Someday she will also be an Educational Ambassador, just like Patch and me!

Mama says that I have touched many lives and changed many people's attitudes toward my species. People from all around the world send me messages and cards – sometimes even gifts. We call them our Opossum Earth Angels!

Being an Educational Ambassador is very important to me. I especially love teaching children about opossums because watching their faces when they pet my soft, silky fur or giggle when I carry bits of paper in my tail, makes me happy. To hear someone yell out, "I love opossums!" makes me so proud. If I could talk, I would shout, "I love children!"

"I love children!"

Opossums are nonaggressive animals that will run away rather than fight. They are gentle and do not carry many diseases so they make perfect Educational Ambassadors.

Even in the best of circumstances, opossums age very quickly and live to only about three years old in the wild. Non-releasable opossums can live longer.

I have been living at Ferncroft for nearly three years. I no longer miss my mother or brothers and sisters. Destiny, Patch, Bella, and all my fans keep me busy.

Now that I am getting older, I sleep more and my beautiful coat is thinning, but thanks to the great care I receive, I just blew out three candles on my birthday cake!

I am such a lucky girl.

I shared my story with you to explain why I live in a house when most wildlife should live in the wild, running happily through the fields and woods. When you share this story, my legacy will live on through you. You can help people understand how special and gentle opossums are. You will become one of our Opossum Earth Angels.

Today, Mama and Papa have packed our travel cages into the car. Patch and I are going to a sanctuary event to teach children and their parents just how special opossums are. I hope someday I will see your face in our audience. Be sure to wave hello and we will smile back at you!

With love,

Lavender

Author's Notes:

I can't think of a time when animals were not a part of my life. As far back as my memory goes, my dad was telling me to be kind to all living things. We named the toad who lived in the rocks and put the praying mantis back where we found it.

When the opportunity to become a Wildlife Rehabilitator presented itself, I jumped at the chance and I have never looked back. It is as though I found the final missing piece of my life's jigsaw puzzle.

This was not a lone journey. I was joined by my husband and partner Bill, who is the kindest and gentlest soul I know. Bill shares my love of animals and together we attended classes, learned about rehabbing, and began planning our on-site rescue.

Ultimately we decided to specialize in opossums. This was the right decision for us. Our main goal is to release animals back to the wild and their natural environment. There is such joy in watching an animal run into the woods looking for a tasty grub or cricket.

Then there was Lavender.

We could not have known how this one little opossum would change our lives.

She arrived at a mere 2 ounces but she filled our minds and hearts. Months of critical care taught us so much. Lavender inspired us, motivated us, and was the impetus for developing education programs to share our passion and knowledge of these gentle creatures.

Today our rescue has grown to include a new rehab clinic and a team of volunteers. Lavender lives in the house with us and can roam freely. As an opossum "elder" she continues to teach us about the life of an opossum. Lavender has taught thousands of people from around the world about these misunderstood animals. She has been an exemplary ambassador.

- Pam

It Takes a Team

A very special thanks goes to Sara Lo Presti, illustrator, whose creative mind and artistic skills brought this book alive. Sara has a BFA in Graphic Design and an MLS in Library Science. She and her husband Michael have been huge fans of opossums for over 25 years. Living in rural northwest Connecticut, she has seen many wild critters wander through her yard, but not one opossum. Yet.

Sara would like to thank her biggest supporters: her husband, daughters Becca and Abby, sister Jane, and dear dear dear friends Tara and Stephanie, as well as Pam and Bill Lefferts for their belief in her and their compassionate care of opossums.

We could not do this without the dedicated medical support provided by Kristen Groves, DVM. Kristen studied, researched and conferred with vets across the country to learn about the care and treatment of opossums. She has taken care of Lavender from the beginning and is not only our vet, she is our teacher and now, our friend.

A graduate of Brown University and the University of Minnesota College of Veterinary Medicine, Kristen truly loves what she does.

I am also grateful for the assistance of Gina Gallois, who patiently mentored and guided me through the publication process. Gina is a former French teacher and lifelong creative-turned-writer and children's book author. Gina is the founder of Moonflower Press. You can purchase Gina's books "Opossum Opposites," "Mama Opossum's Misadventures," and "Cats and Dogs Make the Best of Friends" on Amazon.com.

MOONFLOWER
press

Did you know even more?

1. Opossums have unique defense skills.

   - They open their mouths and show all 50 teeth when they feel threatened. We call this the "opossum smile," which is their first defense to scare you away.

   - Next, they may hiss, growl, and drool. If that doesn't intimidate you, their secret weapon is some of the stinkiest poop you have ever smelled! Phew - I'm outta here!

   - Finally, as a last resort, opossums may "play dead." This is an involuntary coma-like state that can last several hours. Most predators walk away at this point, especially dogs. You may see an opossum that appears dead, but when you go back later to check, she is gone!

2. A group of opossums is a passel. Males are called jacks and females jills. Babies are called joeys.

3. The word opossum comes from the Algonquin Indian name, apasum, meaning "white animal," likely referring to opossums' white faces.

4. Opossums were a favorite of several U.S. presidents.

   - George Washington attempted to send a pair of opossums to a friend in Ireland.

   - Thomas Jefferson played with opossums as a child.

   - Benjamin Harrison had two opossums named Mr. Protection and Mr. Reciprocity for the Republican Party platform at the time.

   - William Taft had a plush opossum made in his honor, called a Billy Possum, to replace the popular Teddy Bear (named after Theodore Roosevelt), but the effort flopped.

   - Herbert Hoover adopted an opossum that had wandered onto the White House grounds and called him Billy Opossum.

Made in the USA
Monee, IL
04 October 2021